Long

Written by Sandra Iversen

This animal is a giraffe.
Giraffes have a long neck.
They have long legs.
They have a long tongue.

long neck

giraffe

long legs

3

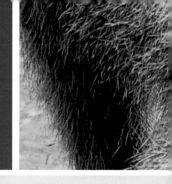

This animal is an anteater.
Anteaters have a long nose.
They have a long tongue.

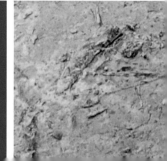

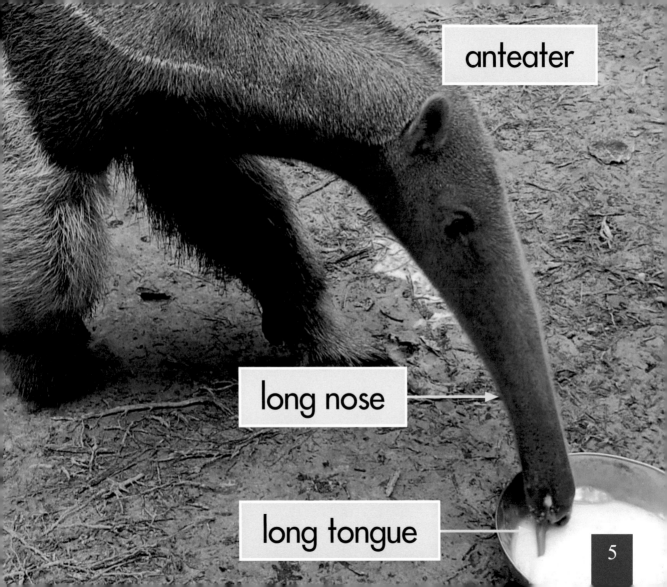

anteater

long nose

long tongue

5

This animal is an elephant.
Elephants have a long trunk.
Look at the long trunk.

elephant

long trunk

7

This animal is a llama.
Llamas have long hair.

llama

long hair

This animal is a monkey
Monkeys like this have long hair.
They have a long tail.

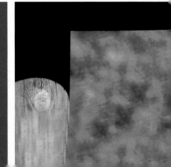

DER MONKEY

long hair

monkey

long tail

Glossary

anteater

elephant

giraffe

llama

monkey